The lost key

Roderick Hunt Alex Brychta

Characters

Narrator
Kipper
Mum/Lady
Boy
Man/Artist
Chip
Biff
Wilma

Casting

This play has eight speaking parts, so that it can be read aloud in a small group. The longer parts are the Narrator and Kipper, and the shorter parts are the Boy and the Man/Artist.

Scene 1

Narrator Scene 1 'Kipper loses the key'
Kipper wanted a magic adventure, but
the magic key wouldn't glow.
It had not glowed for a long time.
He wished and wished for a
magic adventure, but
the key wouldn't glow.

Kipper Maybe the key will glow if I keep it with me.
I'll put it in my pocket.

Mum Kipper! Kipper! Come on!
I want you to come shopping with me.
I want to get you some new trainers.

Narrator On the way to the shops, Mum let Kipper stop and play.
He ran to the rocket and the key fell out of his pocket on to the grass.
At the supermarket Kipper looked in his pockets but the key was not there.

Kipper Where's the key? Oh no! Oh help!
I can't have lost it, can I?
I put it in my pocket. Now it's gone.

Mum What's the matter, Kipper?

Kipper I've lost the key. It must have fallen out of my pocket. It must be by the rocket. We must go and look for it.

Mum It's raining. Ask Biff and Chip to look for it.

Kipper Oh Mum!

Scene 2

Narrator Scene 2 'A man finds the key'
A man came to cut the grass.
The mower ran over the magic key.

(Sound of a loud clang)

Narrator The key broke the mower.
The man was so cross, he threw the magic key in a bin.

(Sound of key falling in the bin)

Narrator Two boys came to play on the swings. One of the boys looked in the bin and found the key.

Boy Look at this old bent key.
Let's tie it to this piece of string.
Then we can spin it round and round.
Like this. See?

(Sound of breaking glass)

Boy Oh no! The string has broken.
The key has hit that man's greenhouse.
It's broken the glass.
Quick! Run for it!

Man Look at my greenhouse!
The glass is broken.
Just you come back here.

Scene 3

Narrator Scene 3 'The children look for the key'
Kipper had to tell Biff and Chip that
he had lost the magic key.

Kipper It fell out of my pocket.
I think I lost it by the rocket.
Mum wouldn't let me look for it.

Chip We must find it.
Come on! We must go and look.

Narrator The children looked for the lost key. But they couldn't find it.

Biff There's the man who cuts the grass. I'll ask him if he's seen the key.

Chip What did he say?

Biff He threw the key in that bin but two boys took it out.

Wilma Look. There they are.

Biff *(shouts)* Have you found an old key?

Boy Yes, but we lost it again.
We broke a man's greenhouse with it.

Wilma Let's ask the man with the greenhouse.

Chip We are sorry about the broken glass.
But could we have the key?

Man Sorry, I sold the key to the junk shop to help pay for the glass.

Narrator The children went to the junk shop. They told the lady about the lost key.

Biff Do you have the key?

Lady Sorry. I have just sold it. A man came in. He wanted some keys. I sold all the keys I had.

Kipper Oh no! How can we find the man?

Lady He has a shop down the street.

Narrator The children went to the man's shop. In the window there were pictures and paintings.

Wilma Why do you think the man wants old keys?

Chip I don't know.

Biff We may have to buy the key back. Let's go home and get some money.

Scene 4

Narrator Scene 4 'Mum buys the key'
Mum went with the children.
She spoke to the man in the shop.
He had painted some pictures and put lots of keys in them.

Mum My children have lost a key.
They think you might have it.
Could they have it back?

Artist Yes, if you can find it.

Narrator The children looked at the pictures but they couldn't see the magic key.

Chip I can't see it anywhere.

Biff All the keys look the same.

Kipper Yippee! Here it is.
It's in this little picture.
This is our key.

Artist Oh yes. I used that key because it was bent.
If you want it you'll have to buy the picture.

Mum How much is it?

Artist It's twenty-five pounds.

Mum It's a lot to pay for an old key!

Scene 5

Narrator Scene 5 'The magic won't work'
That evening, Wilf and Wilma came to the house.
The children pulled the key from the picture and rubbed off the paint.

Biff The key has not glowed for a long time.
Perhaps it has lost its magic.

Wilma It's been out in the rain and it's been bent by a mower.

Chip It's been through a window and it's been stuck on a painting.

Wilma It's had a bad time. Do you think it will ever glow again?

Biff I don't know. I hope so.

Narrator But the key didn't glow and the magic wouldn't work. Kipper told the key about the adventures he would like.

Kipper I want to be like Superman. I'd like to fly . . .

Narrator But still the magic wouldn't work.

Scene 6

Narrator Scene 6 'The children try to make the magic work'
The next day, Wilma came.

Wilma How can we make the magic work?

Chip Let's remind it of the magic adventures. Maybe that will make it work.

Biff Like our visit to the Red Planet.

Kipper Or the time I met the little giant.

Wilma And the time we went small in the garden.

Chip And the time we were in the castle with those horrid witches.

Kipper We've had so many adventures. I hope the key hasn't lost its magic.

Mum It's time to go home, children.
You all look very sad.
What's the matter?

Wilma Nothing.

Mum Well, cheer up, then.

Narrator It was time for bed.
Kipper began to cry.

Kipper I'm sorry about the key.
It's all my fault.
If I hadn't lost the key the magic might work.

Chip Don't cry, Kipper.
Maybe the magic has just run out.

Kipper Oh, I hope not.

Narrator Kipper took the key to bed.
He looked at it for a long time.
At last he fell asleep.
Suddenly the magic key began to glow.

Everyone *(together)* It was time for a new adventure to begin.

Print in China by Imago